*In memory of Lucy Keeling, who edited this book with great skill
and dedication, and who died, sadly, before it was completed.
M.M. and A.K.*

• ◆ •

**For Tracy and the Harries Family,
Thika, Kenya ~ M.M.
To my brother Patrick ~ A.K.**

First American Paperback Edition 2005

First American Edition 2000
by Kane Miller, A Division of EDC Publishing
Tulsa, Oklahoma

This is the Tree copyright © Frances Lincoln Limited 2000
Text copyright © Miriam Moss 2000
Illustrations copyright © Adrienne Kennaway 2000

First published in Great Britain in 2000 by
Frances Lincoln Children's Books
4 Torriano Mews, Torriano Avenue, London NW5 2RZ

All rights reserved. For information contact:
Kane Miller, A Division of EDC Publishing
P.O. Box 470663
Tulsa, OK 74147
www.kanemiller.com

Library of Congress Control Number: 99-049003
Printed and Bound in China

2 3 4 5 6 7 8 9 10

ISBN 978-1-929132-77-5

To Sydney + Elizabeth -

While celebrating Grammie's
70th birthday at Walt Disney World
with "the cousins" - staying at
Kidani Village, AKL. Love, Mommy 3/6-13/10

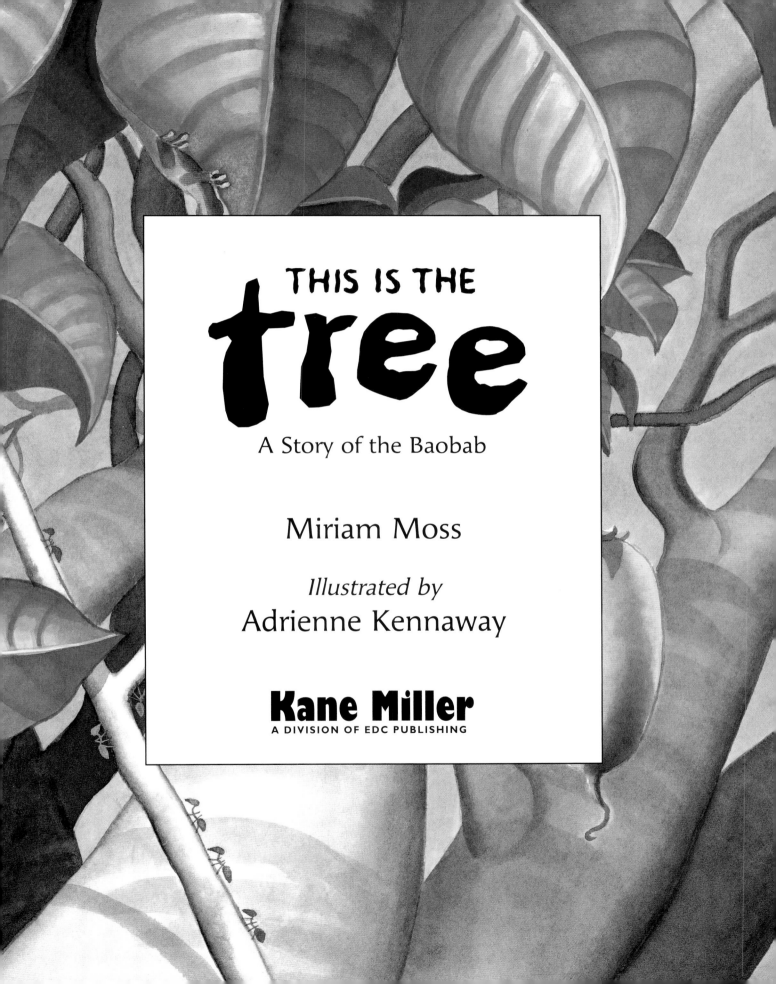

THIS IS THE
tree

A Story of the Baobab

Miriam Moss

Illustrated by
Adrienne Kennaway

Kane Miller
A DIVISION OF EDC PUBLISHING

This is the tree, when the world was still young,
that pushed up through the earth
as a small, tender shoot.

This is the tree, now old as a volcano,
standing alone
on the African plain.

This is the tree with the thousand year roots
that spread out to store water
in a bottle-shaped trunk.

This is the tree where ground squirrel watches
over young, small as mushrooms,
asleep in the roots.

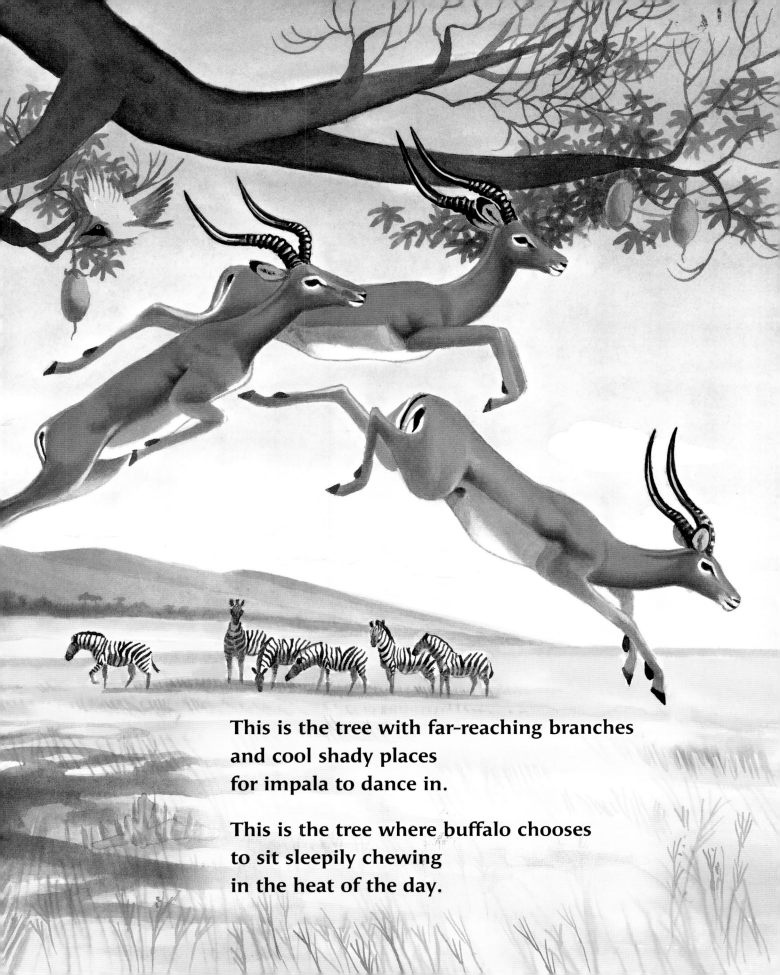

This is the tree with far-reaching branches
and cool shady places
for impala to dance in.

This is the tree where buffalo chooses
to sit sleepily chewing
in the heat of the day.

This is the tree that tosses and turns,
when high winds howl
and the sky turns black.

This is the tree dripping after the storm,
with dark-stained wrinkles
on knuckles and knees.

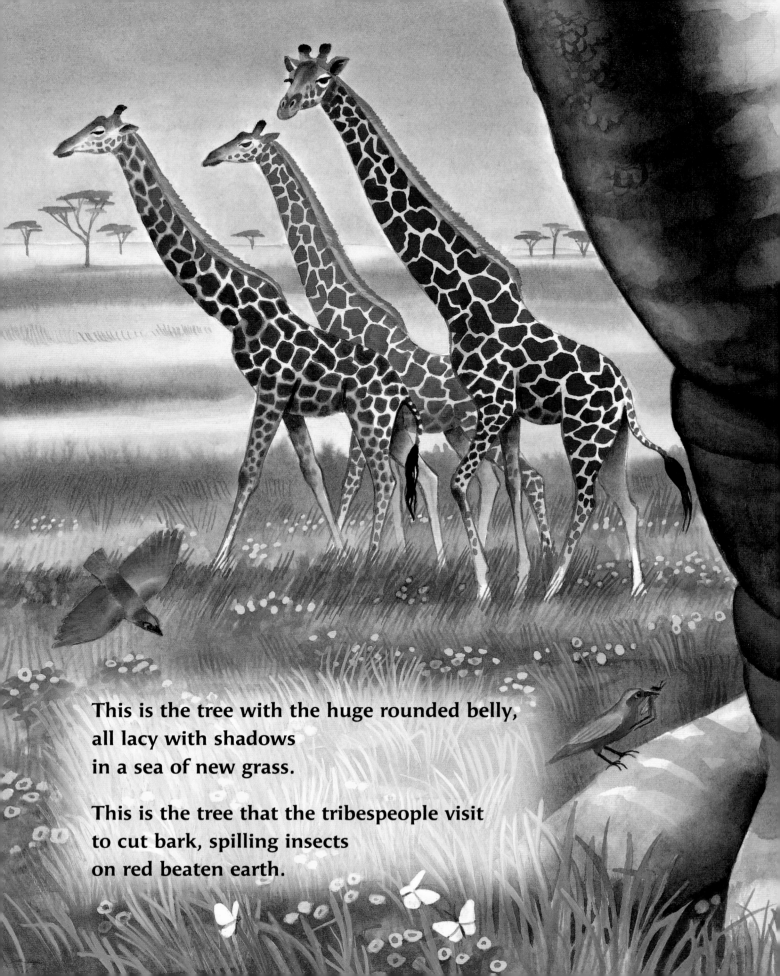

This is the tree with the huge rounded belly,
all lacy with shadows
in a sea of new grass.

This is the tree that the tribespeople visit
to cut bark, spilling insects
on red beaten earth.

This is the tree that is elephant's favorite,
that she scars with rough tusk-marks
to get to the core.

This is the tree a-dangle with fruit pods
that elephant crushes
to slurp up the pulp.

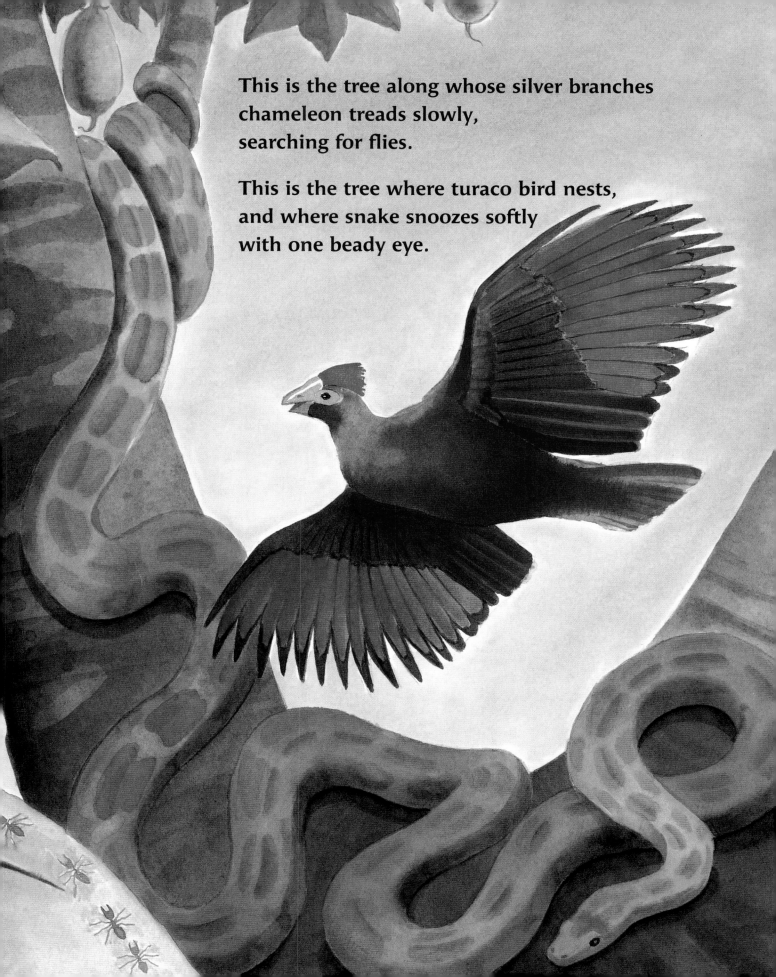

This is the tree along whose silver branches
chameleon treads slowly,
searching for flies.

This is the tree where turaco bird nests,
and where snake snoozes softly
with one beady eye.

This is the tree that bushbaby burgles,
plucking white, waxy petals
with fingers and toes.

This is the tree that dances with monkeys,
alive with their leapings
at the end of the day.

This is the tree where leopard lies darkly,
her eyes only glistening
as bats flitter by.

This is the tree in the silvery moonlight,
that points long crooked toes
to a sharp slice of moon.

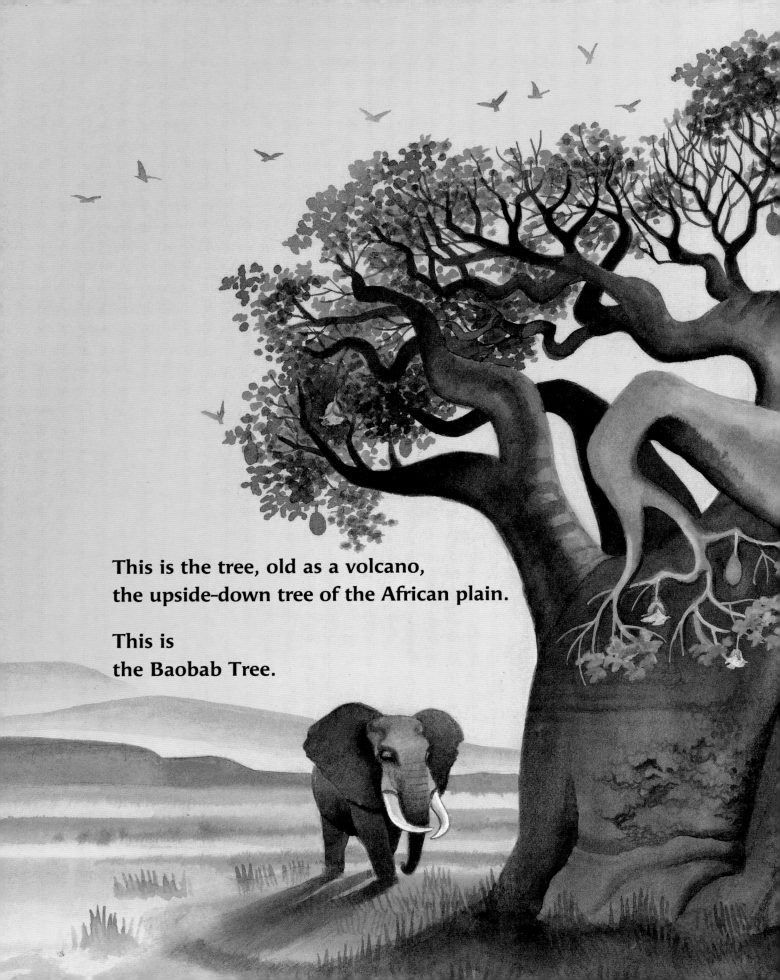

This is the tree, old as a volcano,
the upside-down tree of the African plain.

This is
the Baobab Tree.

The African Baobab is also called the Monkey Bread Tree because baboons love eating its fruit, and the Bottle Tree because of its enormous swollen trunk. 2000-year-old baobabs can have fantastic girths of 10 meters in diameter!

Baobab leaves are not just eaten by cattle, browsing elephants and impala. They are rich in vitamin C and can be cooked like spinach or dried and made into soups and sauces. The leaves are also used as medicine to treat fevers, insect bites and diarrhea.

Baobab flowers are large, white and waxy, with big yellow stamens. They begin to open around sunset but only last until the next morning. They give off a strong rotting smell which attracts bats, bluebottles and nocturnal moths.

Baobab fruits are woody hanging pods, covered in velvety yellow-brown hair. The seeds in ripe fruit are held in place by delicious sweet white pulp that tastes just like wine gums! When the heavy fruits fall from the tree, the woody casing cracks open and termites eat the fruit, leaving the seeds to be carried away by monkeys, baboons, squirrels and rats.

The hollowed-out trunks of baobabs are often used for storing water. A large tree can hold up to 2000 gallons. Hollowed-out baobabs have been used for many weird and wonderful things. They have been prisons, stables, bus shelters, dairies and a weaver's workshop. One baobab tree even had a flush toilet installed in it!

The baobab is home to many other insects and birds in addition to those mentioned in the book. King Baboon spiders, bees, mealy bugs, caterpillars and stick insects all live in the tree. Parrots, hornbills and kingfishers roost or nest in holes in the trunk, while lovebirds, barn owls and Wahlberg's eagles nest in the branches. And, dangling out on the ends of the highest branches, far away from predators, are the little buffalo-weaver birds' round basket nests.

Baobab roots can be cooked and eaten or made into red dye. They are also made into a dried powder to take as a medicine for malaria or as a mouthwash for a toothache.

The strange shape of the baobab has inspired many stories. One says that the first baobab always complained wherever God planted it. In the end God became so fed up that he threw the tree away into the dry soil of the African plain — where it landed upside down! Some say that spirits live in the flowers, so that if you pick a flower, you will be killed by a lion. In Nigeria, religious symbols have been found cut into the bark of ancient trees, suggesting that the trees were worshipped as fertility symbols in the past.

Baobab bark is extraordinary, because when it is cut or damaged it heals itself, just like our skin. Root bark is used to make strings for musical instruments or rope for making fishing nets. In parts of Africa, the fibers are woven into waterproof hats that are also used as drinking cups.

Baobab wood is very spongy as it is full of stored water. It is used to make plates, trays and floats for fishing.